48th Annual Meeting of the Association for Computational Linguistics 2010 (ACL 2010)

Tutorial Abstracts

Uppsala, Sweden
11 July 2010

ISBN: 978-1-61738-829-3

Printed from e-media with permission by:

Curran Associates, Inc.
57 Morehouse Lane
Red Hook, NY 12571

CURRAN ASSOCIATES INC. proceedings.com

Some format issues inherent in the e-media version may also appear in this print version.

Printed by Curran Associates, Inc. (2010)

For permission requests, please contact the Association for Computational Linguistics at the address below.

Association for Computational Linguistics
209 N. Eighth Street
Stroudsburg, Pennsylvania 18360

Phone: 1-570-476-8006
Fax: 1-570-476-0860

acl@aclweb.org

Additional copies of this publication are available from:

Curran Associates, Inc.
57 Morehouse Lane
Red Hook, NY 12571 USA
Phone: 845-758-0400
Fax: 845-758-2634
Email: curran@proceedings.com
Web: www.proceedings.com

Introduction

A total of 20 tutorial proposals were submitted to the ACL 2010 Tutorials track, from which 6 were finally accepted. We are very grateful to the ACL-NLP community for the large amount of exciting, diverse, and high-quality proposals we received. This guaranteed a strong final program, but at the same time made the selection process very difficult. It was really hard to reject some of the proposals. All 20 proposals were reviewed by both co-chairs, and the final selection was approved by the conference General Chair. We also sought expertise from external reviewers where necessary.

Based on the following criteria we selected the maximum number of proposals allowed: 1) Quality: the content and scope of the proposal, and the competence and experience of the presenters; 2) Diversity: We sought a range of different topics and approaches; 3) Appeal: Whether the tutorial topic would be likely to attract a reasonable number of participants; and 4) Novelty: Tutorial topics featured at very recent ACL events were dispreferred (unless the content was clearly novel and different).

The final tutorial programme covers a wide range of NLP topics, including Annotation, Grammars, Discourse Structure, Structured Prediction, Semantic Parsing and Machine Translation.

Sincere thanks to all authors for preparing and sending all the information and materials timely. We know that this is not always easy because of the tight schedule and other competing committments.

We are very indebted to previous tutorial chairs, especially to Diana McCarthy and Chengqing Zong for sharing with us their experience and already developed materials. They provided also valuable advice all throughout the process. We are also equally grateful to the ACL 2010 General Chair, and the Local/Publicity/Publications Chairs for their help and advice in the organization of the Tutorials program and materials, and for sending always the appropriate reminders!

Finally, we only hope that the participation will be as successful as all the previous steps.

To all the attendees, enjoy the ACL 2010 tutorials!

Lluís Màrquez (Technical University of Catalonia, Spain)
Haifeng Wang (Baidu, Inc., China)
ACL 2010 Tutorial Co-Chairs

Tutorial Co-Chairs:

Lluís Màrquez, Technical University of Catalonia, Spain
Haifeng Wang, Baidu, Inc., China

Table of Contents

Tutorial Program

Sunday July 11, 2010

Morning

9:00-12:30 *Wide-Coverage NLP with Linguistically Expressive Grammars*
Julia Hockenmaier, Yusuke Miyao and Josef van Genabith

Tree-Based and Forest-Based Translation
Yang Liu and Liang Huang

Discourse Structure: Theory, Practice and Use
Bonnie Webber, Markus Egg and Valia Kordoni

Afternoon

2:00-5:30 *Annotation*
Eduard Hovy

From Structured Prediction to Inverse Reinforcement Learning
Hal Daumé III

Semantic Parsing: The Task, the State of the Art and the Future
Rohit J. Kate and Yuk Wah Wong

Wide-coverage NLP with Linguistically Expressive Grammars

Julia Hockenmaier
Department of Computer Science,
University of Illinois
juliahmr@illinois.edu

Yusuke Miyao
National Institute of Informatics
yusuke@nii.ac.jp

Josef van Genabith
Centre for Next Generation Localisation,
School of Computing,
Dublin City University
josef@computing.dcu.ie

1 Introduction

In recent years, there has been a lot of research on wide-coverage statistical natural language processing with linguistically expressive grammars such as Combinatory Categorial Grammars (CCG), Head-driven Phrase-Structure Grammars (HPSG), Lexical-Functional Grammars (LFG) and Tree-Adjoining Grammars (TAG). But although many young researchers in natural language processing are very well trained in machine learning and statistical methods, they often lack the necessary background to understand the linguistic motivation behind these formalisms. Furthermore, in many linguistics departments, syntax is still taught from a purely Chomskian perspective. Additionally, research on these formalisms often takes place within tightly-knit, formalism-specific subcommunities. It is therefore often difficult for outsiders as well as experts to grasp the commonalities of and differences between these formalisms.

2 Content Overview

This tutorial overviews basic ideas of TAG/ CCG/LFG/HPSG, and provides attendees with a comparison of these formalisms from a linguistic and computational point of view. We start from stating the motivation behind using these expressive grammar formalisms for NLP, contrasting them with shallow formalisms like context-free grammars. We introduce a common set of examples illustrating various linguistic constructions that elude context-free grammars, and reuse them when introducing each formalism: bounded and unbounded non-local dependencies that arise through extraction and coordination, scrambling, mappings to meaning representations, etc. In the second half of the tutorial, we explain two key technologies for wide-coverage NLP with these grammar formalisms: grammar acquisition and parsing models. Finally, we show NLP applications where these expressive grammar formalisms provide additional benefits.

3 Tutorial Outline

1. Introduction: Why expressive grammars
2. Introduction to TAG
3. Introduction to CCG
4. Introduction to LFG
5. Introduction to HPSG
6. Inducing expressive grammars from corpora
7. Wide-coverage parsing with expressive grammars
8. Applications
9. Summary

References

Aoife Cahill, Michael Burke, Ruth O'Donovan, Stefan Riezler, Josef van Genabith and Andy Way. 2008. Wide-Coverage Deep Statistical Parsing using Automatic Dependency Structure Annotation. *Computational Linguistics*, 34(1). pp.81-124, MIT Press.

Yusuke Miyao and Jun'ichi Tsujii. 2008. Feature Forest Models for Probabilistic HPSG Parsing. *Computational Linguistics*, 34(1). pp.35-80, MIT Press.

Julia Hockenmaier and Mark Steedman. 2007. CCGbank: A Corpus of CCG Derivations and Dependency Structures Extracted from the Penn Treebank. *Computational Linguistics*, 33(3). pp.355-396, MIT Press.

Tutorial Abstracts of ACL 2010, page 1,
Uppsala, Sweden, 11 July 2010.

Tree-based and Forest-based Translation

Yang Liu
Institute of Computing Technology
Chinese Academy of Sciences
yliu@ict.ac.cn

Liang Huang
Information Sciences Institute
University of Southern California
lhuang@isi.edu

1 Introduction

The past several years have witnessed rapid advances in syntax-based machine translation, which exploits natural language syntax to guide translation. Depending on the type of input, most of these efforts can be divided into two broad categories: (a) **string-based systems** whose input is a string, which is simultaneously parsed and translated by a synchronous grammar (Wu, 1997; Chiang, 2005; Galley et al., 2006), and (b) **tree-based systems** whose input is already a parse tree to be directly converted into a target tree or string (Lin, 2004; Ding and Palmer, 2005; Quirk et al., 2005; Liu et al., 2006; Huang et al., 2006).

Compared with their string-based counterparts, tree-based systems offer many attractive features: they are much faster in decoding (linear time vs. cubic time), do not require sophisticated binarization (Zhang et al., 2006), and can use separate grammars for parsing and translation (e.g. a context-free grammar for the former and a tree substitution grammar for the latter).

However, despite these advantages, most tree-based systems suffer from a major drawback: they only use 1-best parse trees to direct translation, which potentially introduces translation mistakes due to parsing errors (Quirk and Corston-Oliver, 2006). This situation becomes worse for resource-poor source languages without enough Treebank data to train a high-accuracy parser.

This problem can be alleviated elegantly by using packed forests (Huang, 2008), which encodes exponentially many parse trees in a polynomial space. Forest-based systems (Mi et al., 2008; Mi and Huang, 2008) thus take a packed forest instead of a parse tree as an input. In addition, packed forests could also be used for translation rule extraction, which helps alleviate the propagation of parsing errors into rule set. Forest-based translation can be regarded as a compromise between the string-based and tree-based methods, while combining the advantages of both: decoding is still fast, yet does not commit to a single parse. Surprisingly, translating a forest of millions of trees is even faster than translating 30 individual trees, and offers significantly better translation quality. This approach has since become a popular topic.

2 Content Overview

This tutorial surveys tree-based and forest-based translation methods. For each approach, we will discuss the two fundamental tasks: *decoding*, which performs the actual translation, and *rule extraction*, which learns translation rules from real-world data automatically. Finally, we will introduce some more recent developments to tree-based and forest-based translation, such as tree sequence based models, tree-to-tree models, joint parsing and translation, and faster decoding algorithms. We will conclude our talk by pointing out some directions for future work.

3 Tutorial Overview

1. Tree-based Translation
    - Motivations and Overview
    - Tree-to-String Model and Decoding
    - Tree-to-String Rule Extraction
    - Language Model-Integrated Decoding: Cube Pruning
2. Forest-based Translation
    - Packed Forest
    - Forest-based Decoding
    - Forest-based Rule Extraction
3. Extensions
    - Tree-Sequence-to-String Models
    - Tree-to-Tree Models
    - Joint Parsing and Translation
    - Faster Decoding Methods
4. Conclusion and Open Problems

Tutorial Abstracts of ACL 2010, page 2,
Uppsala, Sweden, 11 July 2010. ©2010 Association for Computational Linguistics

Discourse Structure: Theory, Practice and Use

Bonnie Webber,♡ Markus Egg,◇ Valia Kordoni♠
♡ University of Edinburgh ◇ Humboldt University ♠ Saarland University
bonnie@inf.ed.ac.uk markus.egg@anglistik.hu-berlin.de kordoni@dfki.de

1 Introduction

This tutorial aims to provide attendees with a clear notion of how discourse structure is relevant for language technology (LT), what is needed for exploiting discourse structure, what methods and resources are available to support its use, and what more could be done in the future.

2 Content Overview

This tutorial consists of four parts. Part I starts with a brief introduction to different bases for discourse structuring, properties of discourse structure that are relevant to LT, and accessible evidence for discourse structure.

For discourse structure to be useful for language technologies, one must be able to automatically recognize or generate with it. Hence, Part II surveys computational approaches to recognizing and generating discourse structure, both manually-authored approaches and ones developed through Machine Learning.

Part III of the tutorial describes applications of discourse structure recognition and generation in LT, as well as discourse-related resources being made available in English, German, Turkish, Hindi, Czech, Arabic and Chinese. Part IV concludes with a list of future possibilities.

3 Tutorial Outline

1. PART I – General Overview
   (a) Bases for structure in monologic, dialogic and multiparty discourse
   (b) Aspects of discourse structure relevant to Language Technology
   (c) Evidence for discource structure
2. PART II – Computational Recognition and Generation of discourse structure
   (a) Discourse chunking and parsing
   (b) Recognizing arguments and sense of discourse connectives
   (c) Recognizing and generating entity-based discourse structure
   (d) Dialogue parsing
3. PART III – Applications and Resources
   (a) Applications to Language Technology
   (b) Discourse structure resources (monolingual and multilingual)
4. PART IV – Future Developments

4 References

○ Regina Barzilay and Lillian Lee (2004). Catching the Drift: Probabilistic Content Models, with Applications to Generation and Summarization. *Proc. 2nd Human Language Technology Conference and Annual Meeting of the North American Chapter, Association for Computational Linguistics*, pp. 113-120.

○ Regina Barzilay and Mirella Lapata (2008). Modeling Local Coherence: An Entity-based Approach. *Computational Linguistics* 34(1), pp. 1-34.

○ Daniel Marcu (2000). *The theory and practice of discourse parsing and summarization*. Cambridge: MIT Press.

○ Umangi Oza, Rashmi Prasad, Sudheer Kolachina, Dipti Misra Sharma and Aravind Joshi (2009). The Hindi Discourse Relation Bank. *Proc. Third Linguistic Annotation Workshop (LAW III)*. Singapore.

○ Rashmi Prasad, Nikhil Dinesh, Alan Lee, Eleni Miltsakaki et al. (2008). The Penn Discourse TreeBank 2.0. *Proc. 6th Int'l Conference on Language Resources and Evaluation*.

○ Manfred Stede (2008). RST revisited: Disentangling nuclearity. In Cathrine Fabricius-Hansen and Wiebke Ramm (eds.), *Subordination versus Coordination in Sentence and Text*. Amsterdam: John Benjamins.

○ Ben Wellner (2008). *Sequence Models and Ranking Methods for Discourse Parsing*. Brandeis University.

○ Deniz Zeyrek, Ümit Deniz Turan, Cem Bozsahin, Ruket Çakici et al. (2009). Annotating Subordinators in the Turkish Discourse Bank. *Proc. Third Linguistic Annotation Workshop (LAW III)*. Singapore.

Tutorial Abstracts of ACL 2010, page 3,
Uppsala, Sweden, 11 July 2010.

Annotation

Eduard Hovy
Information Sciences Institute
University of Southern California
email: hovy@isi.edu

1. Introduction

As researchers seek to apply their machine learning algorithms to new problems, corpus annotation is increasingly gaining importance in the NLP community. But since the community currently has no general paradigm, no textbook that covers all the issues (though Wilcock's book published in Dec 2009 covers some basic ones very well), and no accepted standards, setting up and performing small-, medium-, and large-scale annotation projects remains something of an art.

To attend, no special expertise in computation or linguistics is required.

2. Content Overview

This tutorial is intended to provide the attendee with an in-depth look at the procedures, issues, and problems in corpus annotation, and highlights the pitfalls that the annotation manager should avoid. The tutorial first discusses why annotation is becoming increasingly relevant for NLP and how it fits into the generic NLP methodology of train-evaluate-apply. It then reviews currently available resources, services, and frameworks that support someone wishing to start an annotation project easily. This includes the QDAP annotation center, Amazon's Mechanical Turk, annotation facilities in GATE, and other resources such as UIMA. It then discusses the seven major open issues at the heart of annotation for which there are as yet no standard and fully satisfactory answers or methods. Each issue is described in detail and current practice is shown. The seven issues are: 1. How does one decide what specific phenomena to annotate? How does one adequately capture the theory behind the phenomenon/a and express it in simple annotation instructions? 2. How does one obtain a balanced corpus to annotate, and when is a corpus balanced (and representative)? 3. When hiring annotators, what characteristics are important? How does one ensure that they are adequately (but not over- or under-) trained? 4. How does one establish a simple, fast, and trustworthy annotation procedure? How and when does one apply measures to ensure that the procedure remains on track? How and where can active learning help? 5. What interface(s) are best for each type of problem, and what should one know to avoid? How can one ensure that the interfaces do not influence the annotation results? 6. How does one evaluate the results? What are the appropriate agreement measures? At which cutoff points should one redesign or re-do the annotations? 7. How should one formulate and store the results? When, and to whom, should one release the corpus? How should one report the annotation effort and results for best impact?

The notes include several pages of references and suggested readings.

3. Tutorial Overview

1. Toward a Science of Annotation
   a. What is Annotation, and Why do We Need It?
2. Setting up an Annotation Project
   a. The Basic Steps
   b. Useful Resources and Services
3. Examples of Annotation Projects
4. The Seven Questions of Annotation
   a. Instantiating the Theory
   b. Selecting the Corpus
   c. Designing the Annotation Interface
   d. Selecting and Training Annotators
   e. Specifying the Annotation Procedure
   f. Evaluation and Validation
   g. Distribution and Maintenance
5. Closing: The Future of Annotation in NLP

Tutorial Abstracts of ACL 2010, page 4,
Uppsala, Sweden, 11 July 2010. ©2010 Association for Computational Linguistics

From Structured Prediction to Inverse Reinforcement Learning

Hal Daumé III
School of Computing, University of Utah
and UMIACS, University of Maryland
me@hal3.name

1 Introduction

Machine learning is all about making predictions; language is full of complex rich structure. Structured prediction marries these two. However, structured prediction isn't always enough: sometimes the world throws even more complex data at us, and we need reinforcement learning techniques. This tutorial is all about the *how* and the *why* of structured prediction and inverse reinforcement learning (aka inverse optimal control): participants should walk away comfortable that they could implement many structured prediction and IRL algorithms, and have a sense of which ones might work for which problems.

2 Content Overview

The first half of the tutorial will cover the "basics" of structured prediction: the structured perceptron and Magerman's incremental parsing algorithm. It will then build up to more advanced algorithms that are shockingly reminiscent of these simple approaches: maximum margin techniques and search-based structured prediction.

The second half of the tutorial will ask the question: what happens when our standard assumptions about our data are violated? This is what leads us into the world of reinforcement learning (the basics of which we'll cover) and then to inverse reinforcement learning and inverse optimal control.

Throughout the tutorial, we will see examples ranging from simple (part of speech tagging, named entity recognition, etc.) through complex (parsing, machine translation).

The tutorial does not assume attendees know anything about structured prediction or reinforcement learning (though it will hopefully be interesting even to those who know some!), but *does* assume some knowledge of simple machine learning (eg., binary classification).

3 Tutorial Outline

Part I: Structured prediction

- What is structured prediction?
- Refresher on binary classification
  - What does it mean to learn?
  - Linear models for classification
  - Batch versus stochastic optimization
- From perceptron to structured perceptron
  - Linear models for structured prediction
  - The "argmax" problem
  - From perceptron to margins
- Search-based structured prediction
  - Training classifiers to make parsing decisions
  - Searn and generalizations

Part II: Inverse reinforcement learning

- Refersher on reinforcement learning
  - Markov decision processes
  - Q learning
- Inverse optimal control and A* search
  - Maximum margin planning
  - Learning to search
- Apprenticeship learning
- Open problems

References

See http://www.cs.utah.edu/~suresh/mediawiki/index.php/MLRG/spring10.

Tutorial Abstracts of ACL 2010, page 5,
Uppsala, Sweden, 11 July 2010.

Semantic Parsing: The Task, the State-of-the-Art and the Future

Rohit J. Kate
Department of Computer Science
The University of Texas at Austin
Austin, TX 78712, USA
rjkate@cs.utexas.edu

Yuk Wah Wong
Google Inc.
Pittsburgh, PA 15213, USA
ywwong@google.com

1 Introduction

Semantic parsing is the task of mapping natural language sentences into complete formal meaning representations which a computer can execute for some domain-specific application. This is a challenging task and is critical for developing computing systems that can understand and process natural language input, for example, a computing system that answers natural language queries about a database, or a robot that takes commands in natural language. While the importance of semantic parsing was realized a long time ago, it is only in the past few years that the state-of-the-art in semantic parsing has been significantly advanced with more accurate and robust semantic parser learners that use a variety of statistical learning methods. Semantic parsers have also been extended to work beyond a single sentence, for example, to use discourse contexts and to learn domain-specific language from perceptual contexts. Some of the future research directions of semantic parsing with potentially large impacts include mapping entire natural language documents into machine processable form to enable automated reasoning about them and to convert natural language web pages into machine processable representations for the Semantic Web to support automated high-end web applications.

This tutorial will introduce the semantic parsing task and will bring the audience up-to-date with the current research and state-of-the-art in semantic parsing. It will also provide insights about semantic parsing and how it relates to and differs from other natural language processing tasks. It will point out research challenges and some promising future directions for semantic parsing.

2 Content Overview

The proposed tutorial on semantic parsing will start with an introduction to the task, giving examples of some application domains and meaning representation languages. It will also point out its distinctions from and relations to other NLP tasks. Next, it will talk in depth about various semantic parsers that have been built, starting with earlier hand-built systems to the current state-of-the-art statistical semantic parser learners. It will point out the underlying commonalities and differences between the learners. The next section of the tutorial will talk about the recent advances in extending semantic parsing to work beyond parsing a single sentence. Finally, the tutorial will point out the current research challenges and some promising future directions for semantic parsing.

3 Outline

1. Introduction to the task of semantic parsing
   (a) Definition of the task
   (b) Examples of application domains and meaning representation languages
   (c) Distinctions from and relations to other NLP tasks
2. Semantic parsers
   (a) Earlier hand-built systems
   (b) Learning for semantic parsing
      i. Semantic parsing learning task
      ii. Non-statistical semantic parser learners
      iii. Statistical semantic parser learners
      iv. Exploiting syntax for semantic parsing
      v. Various forms of supervision: semi-supervision, ambiguous supervision
   (c) Underlying commonality and differences between different semantic parser learners
3. Semantic parsing beyond a sentence
   (a) Using discourse contexts for semantic parsing
   (b) Learning language from perceptual contexts
4. Research challenges and future directions
   (a) Machine reading of documents: Connecting with knowledge representation
   (b) Applying semantic parsing techniques to the Semantic Web
   (c) Future research directions
5. Conclusions

Tutorial Abstracts of ACL 2010, page 6,
Uppsala, Sweden, 11 July 2010. ©2010 Association for Computational Linguistics

Author Index